Biographies

Ella Fitzgerald

First Lady of Jazz

by Megan Schoeneberger

Consultant:
Dr. Kyle D. Malone
Assistant Director of Jazz Studies
University of Northern Colorado
Greeley, Colorado

Capstone
press

Mankato, Minnesota

Fact Finders is published by Capstone Press,
151 Good Counsel Drive, P.O. Box 669, Mankato, Minnesota 56002.
www.capstonepress.com

Library of Congress Cataloging-in-Publication Data
Schoeneberger, Megan.
    Ella Fitzgerald: first lady of jazz / by Megan Schoeneberger.
    p. cm.—(Fact finders. Biographies)
    Includes bibliographical references and index.
    ISBN 0-7368-3742-6 (hardcover)
    1. Fitzgerald, Ella—Juvenile literature. 2. Women jazz musicians—United States—
Biography—Juvenile literature. I. Title. II. Series.
ML3930.F5S34 2005
782.42165'092—dc22   2004009816

Summary: A brief introduction to the life of jazz singer Ella Fitzgerald, who recorded more
    than 200 albums and performed at Carnegie Hall 26 times.

Editorial Credits
Donald Lemke, editor; Juliette Peters, set designer; Patrick D. Dentinger, book designer
    and illustrator; Kelly Garvin, photo researcher

Photo Credits
Corbis/Bettmann, cover, 1, 5, 9, 14–15, 16, 17, 23, 24–25, 27; Neal Preston, 26;
    Underwood & Underwood, 20
Getty Images Inc./Hulton Archive, 12, 13, 19, 22
Library of Congress, 6–7, 21; Carl Van Vechten, 11

1 2 3 4 5 6 10 09 08 07 06 05

Table of Contents

Chapter 1

Talent Night

On November 21, 1934, a teenage girl walked onto the stage at the Apollo Theater. It was talent night. The girl was dressed in old clothes and men's boots. She was nervous. She started to sing, but her voice cracked. She stopped.

The audience grew impatient. A few people started to shout and boo. At this contest, members of the crowd booed at dancers and singers who did poorly. They cheered if the performers did well. The act that got the most cheers won the contest.

The Apollo Theater in Harlem, New York, started a talent night for young artists in 1934. ➤

The girl started again. She closed her eyes and sang. This time, her voice floated out over the audience. It filled the theater. When the song ended, the crowd cheered and yelled. Ella Fitzgerald had won first prize.

Chapter 2

Early Life

Ella Jane Fitzgerald was born
on April 25, 1917, in Newport News,
Virginia. Her father, William, left the
family before Fitzgerald's first birthday.
Soon after, Fitzgerald's mother, Tempie,
met Joseph Da Silva. Fitzgerald moved
with the two of them to Yonkers, New
York. Her sister, Frances, was born
in 1923.

FACT!

As a child, Fitzgerald enjoyed
playing baseball. When she grew
up, her favorite baseball team
was the Los Angeles Dodgers.

The train station was the center of Newport News, Virginia, where Fitzgerald was born.

Singing and Dancing

Fitzgerald loved singing. In church, she learned to sing **gospel** music. At home, she sang along with the hits on the radio. Fitzgerald learned to sound like her favorite singers, such as Louis Armstrong and Connee Boswell.

Fitzgerald also loved to dance. She danced as much as she could. Sometimes, Fitzgerald put on dancing shows with her friends. She thought her feet, not her voice, would make her a star.

Rough Times

In 1932, Fitzgerald's mother died from a heart attack. Fitzgerald did not want to live with Da Silva. She moved in with her aunt and cousin in Harlem, New York. Her sister soon joined her.

Fitzgerald was not happy. She dropped out of school and ran away. She made up her mind to become famous in show business.

During the early 1900s, Harlem, New York, was home to many great African American artists.

Chapter 3

A Big Break

On November 21, 1934, Fitzgerald entered a talent contest at the Apollo Theater. She planned to dance. At the last minute, Fitzgerald changed her mind and chose to sing. She won first prize that night. During the next several months, Fitzgerald won many talent contests.

A Chance to Sing

In March 1935, Fitzgerald got her big break. A drummer named Chick Webb was looking for a woman to sing with his band. Webb's saxophone player, Benny Carter, heard Fitzgerald win first prize at the Apollo. Carter found Fitzgerald and brought her to meet Webb.

As a young woman, Fitzgerald was shy when not singing for a crowd.

At first, Webb didn't want to hire Fitzgerald. Her hair was messy. Her clothes were faded and torn. Still, he decided to give her a try. He asked Fitzgerald to sing with his band at their next job. If she did well, he would think about keeping her.

◄ Chick Webb performs on his drums in 1935.

A Diamond in the Rough

Fitzgerald sang with the band for two weeks. Webb liked what he heard. He asked Fitzgerald to sign a contract. She began singing regularly with the band.

Fitzgerald had little experience but learned quickly. It wasn't long before she knew the words and melodies to all of the band's songs. The band members could see her talent.

Fitzgerald sang with the Chick Webb Orchestra at a concert in 1938.

FACT!

Webb looked after Fitzgerald like a father. He helped Fitzgerald find a place to stay and gave her money to buy clothing.

Chapter 4

Highs and Lows

Fitzgerald began making records. She made her first recording on June 12, 1935, with Chick Webb. It was called "Love and Kisses." In 1938, she recorded "A-Tisket, A-Tasket." It was her first hit.

The Chick Webb Orchestra often played at the Savoy Ballroom in Harlem. The Savoy was famous for band battles. During these events, two top bands took turns playing. At the end of the night, the crowd chose the best band.

SAVOY

ERSKINE HAWKINS & TERRY GIBBS
THURSDAY LADIES NIGHT

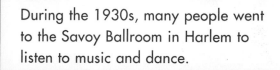

During the 1930s, many people went to the Savoy Ballroom in Harlem to listen to music and dance.

The Chick Webb Orchestra battled the Benny Goodman Orchestra on May 11, 1937. Goodman was the top musician of the year. At least 4,000 people filled the Savoy.

That night, Fitzgerald sang her best. The crowd loved her. They locked arms and swayed to the music. The Chick Webb Orchestra stole the show.

▲ The Benny Goodman Orchestra was a popular jazz band during the 1930s.

F A C T !

When Webb was young, his doctors suggested he learn to play drums. They thought drumming might help Webb's stiff joints caused by his spinal disease.

A Tragic Loss

Meanwhile, Webb's health was poor. He had been born with a disease called spinal tuberculosis. The disease made his legs weak. The horrible pain he had felt throughout his life became worse.

On June 9, 1939, Webb went to the hospital for an operation. He died one week later on June 16. Fitzgerald honored Webb by singing at his funeral.

At Webb's funeral, Fitzgerald (right) helped comfort Webb's wife. ▼

Chapter 5

New Directions

After Webb's death, Fitzgerald took over leading the Chick Webb Orchestra. The band became known as Ella Fitzgerald and Her Famous Orchestra. Fitzgerald became the first woman to lead a **jazz** band. But by 1942, members of the band decided to go their separate ways. They played their last show together at the end of July.

QUOTE

"Just don't give up trying to do what you really want to do. Where there is love and inspiration, I don't think you can go wrong."

—Ella Fitzgerald

After Webb's death, Fitzgerald performed with other musicians, including drummer Bill Beason.

Scat Singing

By 1942, Fitzgerald had made 150 records. Soon, she became interested in a new kind of music called **bebop**. This type of jazz uses **scat** singing. In scat, singers use their voices to sound like musical instruments.

Soon, Fitzgerald started recording scat songs. In "Flying Home," Fitzgerald used words, syllables, and parts of other songs to scat. Fitzgerald became known as one of the best scat singers of her time.

◄ During the 1940s, Fitzgerald became known as one of the best scat singers.

Fitzgerald's ➤
music played on
radio stations
across the
United States.

QUOTE

"I stole everything
I ever heard, but
mostly I stole from
the horns."
   —Ella Fitzgerald

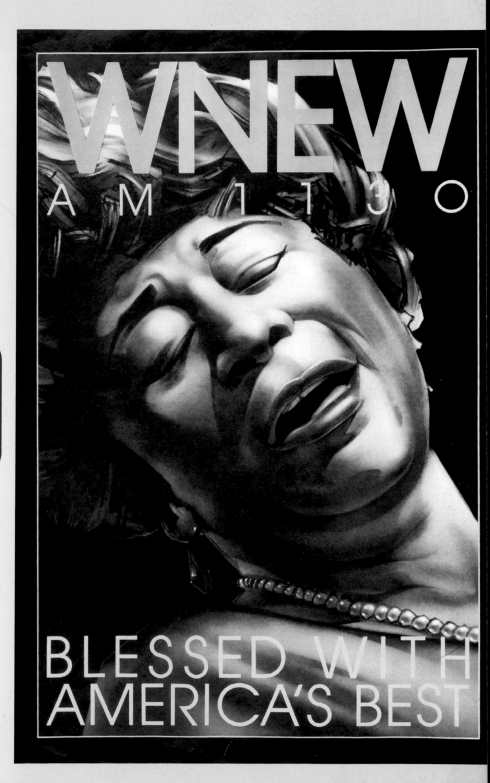

WNEW
AM 1130

BLESSED WITH
AMERICA'S BEST

In November 1946, Fitzgerald went on tour with Dizzy Gillespie, a famous bebop musician. While on tour, she met a bass player named Ray Brown. Fitzgerald and Brown married in 1947. The couple adopted a son, Ray Jr., a short time later. Fitzgerald and Brown divorced on August 28, 1953.

Fitzgerald and bass player Ray Brown were married from 1947 to 1953.

The Songbooks

In 1956, Fitzgerald recorded the first of a series of **songbooks**. In these song collections, Fitzgerald sang music from famous American **composers**. They included George and Ira Gershwin, Cole Porter, and Duke Ellington.

Fitzgerald performed with jazz great Duke Ellington in 1970. ▼

Chapter 6

The End of the Song

As she grew older, Fitzgerald continued performing and recording. In the 1970s, she performed with large orchestras. By 1991, she had performed at Carnegie Hall 26 times. She had recorded at least 200 albums.

In her final years, Fitzgerald's health was poor. Her eyesight was failing. In 1986, she had heart surgery. Doctors discovered she had **diabetes**. In 1993, they had to remove both of her legs because of poor blood flow. Fitzgerald stopped appearing in public after the operation. On June 15, 1996, she died at her home in Beverly Hills, California. She was 79 years old.

On July 5, 1973, Fitzgerald performed at Carnegie Hall with members of the Chick Webb Orchestra.

Fitzgerald continued singing ▲ into the early 1990s.

Chick Webb once warned Fitzgerald not to rise to the top too fast. By building her fame slowly, he said, she would stay on top longer. For more than 60 years, Fitzgerald sang all kinds of music. But most of all, she sang jazz. Today, many people fall in love with jazz music because of Fitzgerald. She is still on top.

QUOTE

"The only thing better than singing is more singing."
—Ella Fitzgerald

Fast Facts

Full name: Ella Jane Fitzgerald

Nickname: First Lady of Song

Occupation: Singer

Birth: April 25, 1917

Death: June 15, 1996

Hometown: Newport News, Virginia

Parents: William and Tempie Fitzgerald

Siblings: one sister, Frances

Son: Ray Jr.

First stage performance: Amateur Night at the
    Apollo Theater, 1934

First recording: "Love and Kisses," 1935

First number one hit:
    "A-Tisket, A-Tasket," 1938

Number of albums: At least 200

Time Line

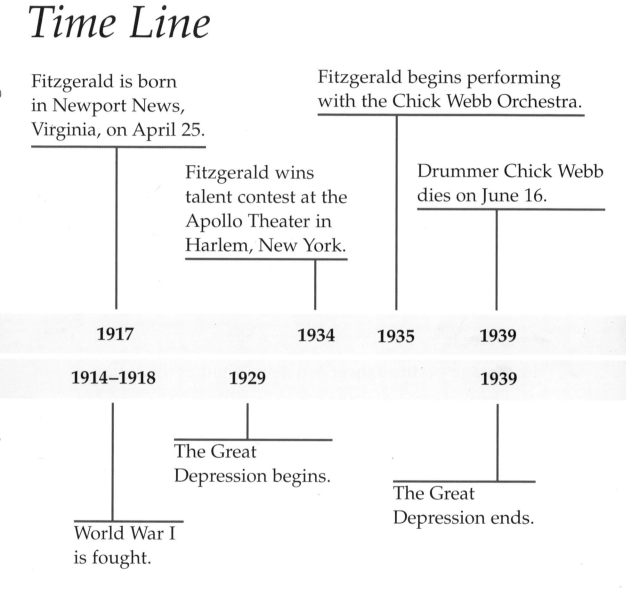

Life Events of Ella Fitzgerald

Fitzgerald is born in Newport News, Virginia, on April 25.

Fitzgerald begins performing with the Chick Webb Orchestra.

Fitzgerald wins talent contest at the Apollo Theater in Harlem, New York.

Drummer Chick Webb dies on June 16.

1917   **1934**   **1935**   **1939**

1914–1918   **1929**   **1939**

Events in U.S. History

The Great Depression begins.

World War I is fought.

The Great Depression ends.

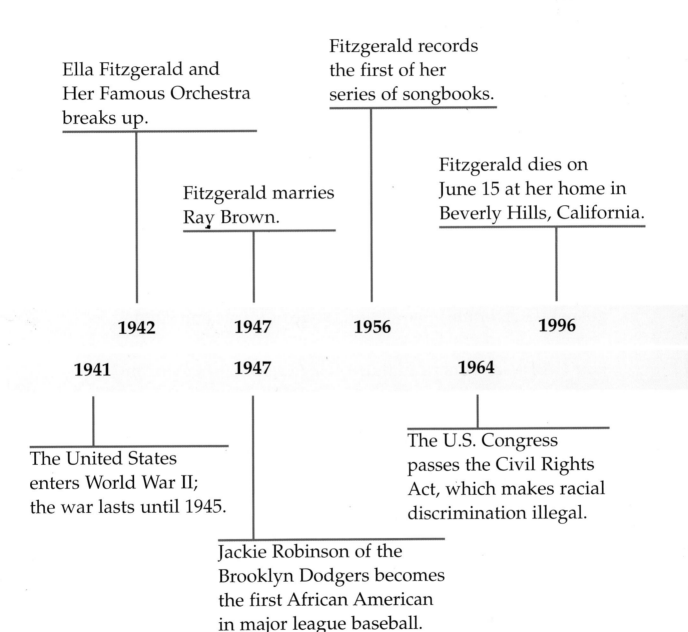

Ella Fitzgerald and Her Famous Orchestra breaks up.

Fitzgerald records the first of her series of songbooks.

Fitzgerald marries Ray Brown.

Fitzgerald dies on June 15 at her home in Beverly Hills, California.

1942

1947

1956

1996

1941

1947

1964

The United States enters World War II; the war lasts until 1945.

The U.S. Congress passes the Civil Rights Act, which makes racial discrimination illegal.

Jackie Robinson of the Brooklyn Dodgers becomes the first African American in major league baseball.

Glossary

bebop (BEE-bahp)—a complex, fast-paced type of jazz music played by small jazz groups

composer (kuhm-POZE-uhr)—a person who writes songs or music

diabetes (dye-uh-BEE-teez)—a disease in which there is too much sugar in the blood

gospel (GOSS-puhl)—a religious style of music and singing

jazz (JAZ)—an American musical style combining African, American, and western European music

scat (SKAT)—a type of singing in which the singer imitates a jazz instrument vocally without words

songbook (SAWNG-buk)—a collection of recorded songs

Internet Sites

FactHound offers a safe, fun way to find Internet sites related to this book. All of the sites on FactHound have been researched by our staff.

Here's how:

1. Visit *www.facthound.com*
2. Type in this special code: **0736837426** for age-appropriate sites. Or enter a search word related to this book for a more general search.
3. Click on the **Fetch It** button.

FactHound will fetch the best sites for you!

Read More

Brasch, Nicolas. *Jazz and Blues.* Music. North Mankato, Minn.: Smart Apple Media, 2004.

Martin, Marvin. *Extraordinary People in Jazz.* Extraordinary People. New York: Children's Press, 2004.

Pinkney, Andrea Davis. *Ella Fitzgerald: The Tale of a Vocal Virtuosa.* New York: Jump at the Sun/Hyperion Books for Children, 2002.

Index